KAPIL DEV

KAPIL DEV
by **KAPIL DEV**

Published by

Delhi Open Books

G/F, 4771/23, Bharat Ram Road, Daryaganj, New Delhi-110002
Ph.: 91-11-42408081
E-mail: delhiopenbooks2016@gmail.com

ISBN: 9789389847376

Cover, Typesetting, and Book Design by ROHIT

Kapil Dev Ram Lal Nikhanj (born 6 January 1959) is a former Indian cricketer. He was a fast bowler and a hard hitting middle order batsman. Regarded as one of the greatest all-rounders to play the game, he is also regarded as one of the greatest captains in the history of cricket. He was named by Wisden as the Indian Cricketer of the Century in 2002. Dev captained the Indian cricket team that won the 1983 Cricket World Cup. He was India's national cricket coach between October 1999 and August 2000. He retired in 1994, holding the world record for the greatest number of wickets taken in Test cricket, a record subsequently broken by Courtney Walsh in 2000. At the time, he was also India's highest wicket taker in both major forms of cricket, Tests and ODIs. He is the first player to take 200 ODI wickets. He is the only player in the history of cricket to have taken more than 400 wickets (434 wickets) and scored more than 5000 runs in Tests, making him one of the greatest all-rounders to have played the game. On 11 March 2010, Dev was inducted into the ICC Cricket Hall of Fame.

Contents

Early life	**2**
Domestic career	**3**
Captain: 1983 World Cup champions (1982–1984)	**7**
1983 World Cup	**8**
Post-World Cup	**10**
Final years	**11**
Personal life	**12**
Captaincy & Record	**13**
Test Matches	**15**
Records:	**16**
Awards	**17**

Kapil Dev captained the Indian cricket team that won the 1983 Cricket World Cup (Officially The Prudential Cup-1983) in England. He retired in 1994, holding the world record for the Highest number of wickets taken in Test cricket & One Day Internationals (At the time of His Retirement), a record subsequently broken by Courtney Walsh in 2000 in Test Matches. At the time, he was also India's highest wicket taker in both ODI & Test cricket. He is the only player in the history of cricket to have taken more than 400 wickets (434 wickets) and scored more than 5000 runs in Tests (5,248 Runs In Test), making him one of the greatest all-rounders to have played the game. He was India's national cricket coach between October 1999 and August 2000. On 11 March 2010, Dev was inducted into the ICC Cricket Hall of Fame.

Early life

Kapil Dev was born as Kapil Dev Nikhanj to Ram Lal Nikhanj, and his wife Raj Kumari Ram Lal Nikhanj in Chandigarh on 6 January 1959. His father was from Dipalpur. They lived in Shah Yakka which is now in Okara district, Pakistan. Kapil Dev was a student at D.A.V. School and joined Desh Prem Azad in 1971 (Former Indian Cricketer & Coach).

Domestic career

Haryana

Kapil Dev made an impressive debut for Haryana in November 1975 against Punjab with a 6 wicket haul, restricting Punjab to 63 runs and helping Haryana to victory. He finished the season with 121 wickets in 30 matches.

In the 1976–77 season opener against Jammu & Kashmir, he had a match haul of 8/36 in the win. Helping Haryana to qualify for the pre-quarterfinals. Kapil Dev achieved his then best innings haul of 8/20 in just 9 overs in the second innings to Bowled Out Bengal for 58 runs in under 19 overs. Haryana lost the quarter finals to Bombay. Bombay won the Season by Beating Delhi in the finals by 129 Runs.

He began his 1977–78 season claiming 8/38 in the first innings against Services. With 3 wickets in the second innings, he took his maiden 10-wicket haul in first-class cricket, a feat he would later achieve twice in Test cricket. With 23 wickets in 4 matches, he was selected for the Irani Trophy, Duleep Trophy and Wills Trophy matches.

In the 1978–79 season, Haryana played Bengal in the pre-quarterfinal match.In the pre-quarterfinal match, Kapil Dev took a 5-wicket haul in the first innings. Poor batting by Haryana in the second innings let Bengal avenge their loss from 2 seasons back by scoring the required 161 runs for the loss of just 4 wickets. Kapil Dev stood out in the Irani Trophy match, scoring 62 runs coming in at number 8. He took 5 wickets in the game where Karnataka was defeated by the Rest of India XI by 9 Wickets. Kapil Dev arrived in the national spotlight with a standout performance in the finals of the Duleep Trophy, taking a first innings haul of 7/65 in 24 overs and 4 Maiden Overs. He was included in the North Zone squad for Deodhar Trophy and Wills Trophy. He played his first Test match in the season against Pakistan.

In the 1979–80 season, Kapil Dev showed his batting talent with a maiden century against Delhi when he scored his career best 193. In the pre-quarterfinal match, where he captained Haryana for the first time against Uttar Pradesh, he took a five wicket haul in the second innings to advance to quarterfinals, where they lost to Karnataka. Delhi Defeated Bombay in the final by 240 Runs.

In the 1990–91 Ranji season, Haryana reached semi-finals on the back of the bowling performance of Chetan Sharma and the batting performance of Amarjit Kaypee. Kapil Dev took centre stage in the semi-final against Bengal, where he led his team to a Mammoth score of 605 runs by scoring 141 as well as taking 5 wickets and conceding 85 Runs.

Ranji final of the 1991 season will be remembered for the number of international cricketers who participated, including Kapil Dev, Chetan Sharma, Ajay Jadeja and Vijay Yadav representing Haryana and Bombay cricket team represented by Sanjay Manjrekar, Vinod Kambli, Sachin Tendulkar, Dilip Vengsarkar, Chandrakant Pandit, Salil Ankola and Abey Kuruvilla. Deepak Sharma (199 Runs), Ajay Jadeja (94 Runs) and Chetan Sharma (98 Runs) helped Haryana to a score of 522 while Yogendra Bhandari (5 wickets) and Kapil Dev (3 wickets) restricted Bombay to 410 runs in the first innings. A crucial 41 from Kapil Dev and top scorer Ajay Banerjee (60) took Haryana to 242 runs, setting Bombay a target of 355 runs. After the 3 Quick wickets, Dilip Vengsarkar (139 Runs) and Sachin Tendulkar (96 Runs) fought back for the Bombay team. After Sachin

Tendulkar's dismissal, Haryana took the final 6 wickets for 102 runs and Haryana Winning the Finals by 2 Runs. Kapil Dev won his maiden and only Ranji Trophy championship.

International career (1978-1982)

Kapil Dev made his Test cricket debut in Faisalabad, Pakistan on 16 October 1978. Kapil Dev captured his maiden wicket of Sadiq Mohammad with his trademark outswinger. He showcased his all-rounder talent when he scored half-century off 33 balls and 2 sixes in each of the innings during the 3rd Test match at National Stadium, Karachi, although India lost the match and the series 2–0.The series against a visiting West Indies team, he scored his maiden Test century (126) at Feroz Shah Kotla, Delhi in just 124 balls and had a steady bowling performance (17 wickets).In his first series outside the sub-continent against England, He picked up his first 5-wicket haul and all of England's wickets, although it came at a huge cost (48 overs and 146 runs conceded) as England scored a mammoth 633 and won the match comfortably. Kapil Dev finished the series with 16 wickets. His debut in ODI Cricket happened in the earlier tour of Pakistan.

Kapil Dev established himself as India's premier fast bowler when he took two 5-wicket hauls and ended the home series against Australia with 28 wickets (Average: 22.32) and also 212 runs that included a half-century and Helping India winning the series 2-0.He gained fame in the 6-Test home series against Pakistan in the 1979–80 season when he led India to 2 victories against the visitors – once with the bat (69) at Wankhede Stadium, Bombay (India won the match by 131 Runs) and the second time with bat and ball (10-wicket haul in match – 4/90 in the first innings and 7/56 in the second innings, 84 in 98 balls with his bat) at Chepauk, Madras (Now Chennai) helping India won by 10 Wickets.

India's tour of Australia in 1980–81 had the looks of the familiar Indian series as India were 1–0 down and were defending a meagre 143 runs and Kapil Dev virtually ruled out with a groin injury. When Australia finished the fourth day at 18/3, Dev willed himself to play the final day with pain-killing injections and removed the dangerous Australia middle order (Wickers of B Yardly, A Border, R Marsh, D Lillee & J Higgs). Dev won the match for India with the innings bowling performance of 16.4–4–28–5, a bowling performance that figures in his five best bowling performance.

Kapil Dev was ready for the 1981–82 home series against England where his five-wicket haul won the first test at Wankhede Stadium, Bombay. He scored 318 runs (Average: 53, 1 century, 1 fifty) and took 22 wickets (2 5-wicket hauls) and walked away with the Man of the Series award. England saw more of Dev in the ensuing series at home against the Indian cricket team in the 1982 season when he opened with a 5-wicket haul and 130 runs in a losing cause at Lord's. He finished the 3-match series with 292 runs (Ave: 73, 3 fifties) and 10 Wickets and bagged the Man of the Series again.

Facing Sri Lanka for the first time, Kapil Dev helped himself to a five-wicket haul to kick start the 1982–83 season. In the following tour to Pakistan, Kapil Dev and Mohinder Amarnath were the only bright spots in a series dominated by rival all-rounder Imran Khan (40 wickets and 1 century). Kapil Dev took a 5/102 haul in the second Test at National Stadium, Karachi, 7/220 in the third Test at Iqbal Stadium, Faisalabad and 8/85 at Gaddafi Stadium, Lahore while he received little support from other team members. After this disastrous tour, Kapil Dev was made the captain of the Indian cricket team in place of Sunil Gavaskar.

Captain: 1983 World Cup champions (1982–1984)

Kapil Dev debuted as India's captain in the 1982–83 season against Sri Lanka in ODI Series (before the Pakistan tour) when Sunil Gavaskar was rested. His first assignment as regular captain was the tour of West Indies, where the biggest accomplishment was a ODI victory. Kapil Dev (72) and Gavaskar (90) led India to a huge score – 282/5 in 47 overs and Dev's 2 wickets aided India to restrict West Indies for 255 and winning by 27 Runs.Indian cricketers claim gave them the confidence to face the West Indies team in 1983 Cricket World Cup.

1983 World Cup

India's solitary victory in the previous two World Cups was against East Africa in 1975. India Played West Indies in 1st match, Riding on Yashpal Sharma's (89 Runs), Roger Binny and Ravi Shastri's (3 wickets each) helped India beating West Indies by 34 Runs. This was first-ever defeat in the World Cup for West Indies. Following a victory against Zimbabwe, India lost the next two matches to Australia and West Indies. India now needed victories against Australia and Zimbabwe to advance to the semi-finals.

India faced Zimbabwe at Nevill Ground, Royal Tunbridge Wells on 18 June 1983. India lost 5 wickets with score being 17 Runs, Kapil Dev batting with the lower order batsmen, stabilised the side with help from Roger Binny (22 runs), Partnership of 60 Runs and with Madan Lal (17 Runs), partnership of 62 Runs. Kapil Dev scored his century off 100 balls. Together with Wicket Keeper Syed Kirmani (22 runs), They put on an unbeaten 126 runs for the 9th wicket – a world record that stood unbroken for almost 27 years, and finished not out with 175 runs off 138 balls, an innings that included 16 boundaries and 6 sixes. The innings figures in the Top 10 ODI Batting Performances at No. 4. India won the match by 31 runs.

In the semifinals India faced the English cricket team. Kapil Dev helped curtail the lower order after England lost regular wickets to R Binny and M Amarnath. He took 3 wickets as India limited England to 213 and the middle order of M Amarnath (46 runs), Yashpal Sharma (61) and Sandeep Patil (51*) ensured victory and entry into the finals to take on the West Indies cricket team who were looking for a hat-trick of World Cup titles (They had won the previous two World Cup's). West Indies restricted India for 183 runs, with Krishnamachari Srikkanth (38 runs) & Sandeep Patil (27 Runs), Mohinder Amarth (26 Runs) providing some scoring relief. Despite losing Gordon Greenidge for 1 Run, West Indies steadied their innings to 57/2 on the back of quick scoring by Viv Richards. Viv Richards played one too many aggressive shots when he skied a pull shot from Madan Lal that Kapil Dev caught at deep square leg after running backwards for over 18 Metres. The catch is attributed as the turning point in the 1983 World Cup Final and is regarded as one of the finest in ODI Cricket. West Indies collapsed and finally were bowled out for 140 with Kapil Dev picking up the wicket of Andy Roberts. Kapil Dev led with 303 runs (Average: 60.6), 12 wickets (Average: 20.41) and 7 catches in 8 matches.

Post-World Cup

After the World Cup, India hosted the West Indies cricket team and lost the Test series 3–0 and the ODI Series 5–0. Dev achieved his best test bowling performance at Motera Stadium, Ahmedabad with a bowling performance of 9/83.

He was retained as captain for the 1987 Cricket World Cup. In their first match, Australia scored 268 against India. However, after the close of innings, Kapil Dev agreed with the umpires that the score should be increased to 270 as one boundary during the innings had been mistakenly signalled as a four and not a six. In their reply, India scored 269 falling short of Australia's score by one run. India went on to reach the semi-final of the 1987 World Cup, where they lost to England by 35 Runs. He did not captain India again, although he was the Vice-captain for India's tour to Pakistan in 1989. Australia won the 1987 World Cup by defeating England in the final by 7 Runs.

Final years

Kapil Dev continued as India's lead pace bowler under a succession of captains in the early 1990s. He was involved in a notable incident during the Lord's Test Match of 1990, when he hit off-spinner Eddie Hemmings for four sixes in 4 Balls to take India past the follow-on target. This match featured the highest test score by an Englishman against India, 333 by Graham Gooch.

Kapil Dev was cited by umpire Dickie Bird as being one of the greatest all-rounders of all-time.

He played in the 1992 Cricket World Cup, his last, under the captaincy of Mohammad Azharuddin. He led the bowling attack with younger talents like Javagal Srinath and Manoj Prabhakar, who would eventually succeed him as India's leading pace bowlers. He retired in 1994, after breaking Richard Hadlee's then standing record for the most Test wickets taken.

Personal life

He married Romi Bhatia in 1980 and had a daughter, Amiya Dev, Born on 16 January 1996.

In 1994, Kapil Dev took up golf. Dev was the only Asian founding member of Laureus Foundation in 2000. Ian Botham and Viv Richards were the other two cricketers on the founding member council of 40. Steve Waugh was added to the Academy members in 2006 when it was expanded from 40 to 42.

He pledged his organs during an event organized by Delhi Urological Society on January 31, 2014 at the Airport Authority of India, Officers Club, New Delhi.

Captaincy & Record

One Day Internationals

Opposition	Matches	Won	Lost	Tied	NR
Australia	19	9	9	0	1
England	5	3	2	0	0
New Zealand	8	6	2	0	0
Pakistan	13	4	9	0	0
Sri Lanka	13	10	2	0	1
West Indies	12	3	9	0	0
Zimbabwe	4	4	0	0	0
Total	74	39	33	0	2

Records:

• Highest wicket-taker in ODI cricket (1978-1994) with a career tally of 253 wickets at the time of Retirement.

• Peak rating (631) is the highest ever achieved (22 March 1985) after a World Series final against Pakistan in Australia. (India won the World Series by Defeating Pakistan in final by 8 wickets).

• Highest ODI score when batting at number 6 position or lower as well in World Cup history(175 Not Out).

• Most number of balls in an ODI innings when batting at number six position in ODI history(138, tied with Neil McCallum)

Test Matches

Opposition	Matches	Won	Lost	Tied	Draw
Austraia	6	0	0	1	5
England	3	2	0	0	1
Pakistan	8	0	1	0	7
Sri Lanka	6	2	1	0	3
West Indies	11	0	5	0	6
Total	34	4	7	1	22

Records:

- In early 1994, he became the highest Test wicket-taker in the world, breaking the record held by Sir Richard Hadlee. Kapil Dev's record was broken by Courtney Walsh in 1999.
- Only player to have achieved the all-rounder's double of 4,000 Test runs and 400 Test wickets
- Most innings in a career (184) without being run out.
- Youngest test cricketer to take 100 (21 years, 25 days), 200 (24 years, days) and 300 wickets(27 years, 2 days)
- Best bowling figures in an innings of a test match as captain (9/83) and in fact, he is the only captain to take a 9 wicket haul in a test innings.
- Best bowling in a test innings in a losing cause(9/83).

Awards

- 1979–80 – Arjuna Award
- 1982 – Padma Shri
- 1983 – Wisden Cricketer of the Year
- 1991 – Padma Bhushan
- 2002 – Wisden Indian Cricketer of the Century
- 2010 – ICC Cricket Hall of Fame
- 2012-2013 CK Nayudu Lifetime Achievement award

9 789389 847376

Printed by Libri Plureos GmbH in Hamburg,
Germany